CONTENTS

FROM THE EDITOR

Charmeachealle "Mike" Moore is our featured superstar this month.

Mike was a linebacker in the NFL, playing for the Los Angeles Chargers. But what's even more exciting for us is the positive change he's making with his organization, We L;ving (pronounced We Living).

We L;ving serves as a voice for the voiceless and empowers schools and communities to reach their full potential. You can learn more in Mike's feature article in this issue.

We also welcome the following great authors this month:

Luba Sakharuk of RALM3 talks about transform yourself and others through mentorship.

David Wolf of Audivita teaches us how to maximize your message.

Scott Sery, badass copywriter from Billings, MT, tells us what nobody told him about entrepreneurship.

PIVOT Magazine

Founder and President
Jason Miller
jason@strategicadvisorboard.com

Editor-in-Chief
Chris O'Byrne
chris@jetlaunch.net

Design
JETLAUNCH.net

Advertising
Chris O'Byrne
chris@jetlaunch.net

Webmaster
Joel Phillips
joel@proshark.com

Editor
Laura West
laura@jetlaunch.net

Cover Design
Debbie O'Byrne

FROM THE DESK OF THE PRESIDENT

Strategies for Leading Change Effectively

Jason Miller

Leading change effectively is a critical component of leadership in the business world. With the ever-evolving market conditions, technological advancements, and changes in consumer behavior, the ability to successfully implement change can mean the difference between a thriving business and a struggling one. Companies that can lead change effectively are often those that are well-positioned to grow, innovate, and stay ahead of the competition. However, change can be a challenging process for many people, including employees and stakeholders, who often face feelings of uncertainty and a loss of control. As a result, it is crucial for leaders to lead change effectively to ensure that the desired outcomes are achieved, and the process is as smooth as possible.

The following strategies can help leaders lead change effectively:

1. Develop a clear vision

Leaders must have a clear vision of the change they want to implement and the desired outcome. This vision should be communicated in a clear and concise manner to all stakeholders involved. A clear vision helps align everyone towards a common goal and provides everyone with a clear understanding of the changes being made. Leaders should take the time to consider the desired outcome, the impact the change will have on all stakeholders, and the resources required to make the change a reality. This ensures that everyone is working towards the same goal and provides a roadmap for success.

2. Engage all stakeholders

Change can be daunting for some people, and it is essential to engage all stakeholders in the process. This includes employees, customers, suppliers, and other key stakeholders. Engaging stakeholders in the change process can help reduce resistance and ensure that everyone is on board. This can be done through regular communication, open forums, and feedback from stakeholders. Regular engagement helps build trust and ensures that everyone is informed and aware of the changes being made.

3. Communicate regularly

Clear and effective communication is key to successful change. Leaders must communicate regularly with all stakeholders to provide updates and answer any questions they may have. Communication helps build trust and ensures that everyone is informed and aware of the changes being made. Leaders should also listen to feedback from stakeholders and be open to modifying the change process if necessary. This helps ensure that the change process is on track and that any issues are addressed quickly and effectively.

4. Empower employees

Change can result in a loss of control, which can be unsettling for employees. Leaders must empower employees to take control of their own work and help them feel that they are making a positive contribution to the change process. This can be done through training and development opportunities and by providing employees with the resources they need to succeed. Empowering employees helps build a sense of ownership and responsibility, which can increase motivation and engagement in the change process.

5. Lead by example

Leaders must lead by example and show their commitment to the change process. This can be done by actively participating in the change process, leading from the front, and demonstrating a positive attitude toward the change. Leading by example sets a positive tone and helps inspire others to get involved. It is also essential for leaders to be transparent and honest about the change process, as this helps build trust and confidence in their leadership.

6. Be flexible and adaptable

Change can be unpredictable, and leaders must be flexible and adaptable to the changes that may arise. This requires a willingness to learn and a flexible mindset, which can be achieved through training and development opportunities. Leaders must also be open to feedback and willing to modify their approach as necessary. A flexible and adaptable leadership style helps ensure that the change process is on track and that any issues can be addressed quickly and effectively.

7. Measure progress

Leaders must measure progress regularly and make adjustments as needed. This can be done by setting clear milestones and tracking progress against them. Regular progress updates help ensure that the change process is on track and that desired outcomes are being achieved. It also helps to identify any challenges or obstacles that may arise, allowing leaders to adjust their approach as necessary. Progress tracking can be done through regular meetings with stakeholders, progress reports, and feedback from employees. This helps ensure that everyone is informed and aware of the progress being made and that the change process remains on track.

8. Encourage risk-taking

Change often requires taking risks, and leaders must encourage employees to take risks and embrace new ideas. This can be done by creating a culture of innovation, where employees feel empowered to suggest new ideas and take risks in their work. Encouraging risk-taking helps create an environment where new ideas and innovation can flourish and where employees are motivated to contribute to the change process.

9. Foster a positive work environment

Leaders must foster a positive work environment where employees feel supported and valued. This can be done by creating a culture of trust, open communication, and collaboration. A positive work environment helps employees feel motivated and engaged, which can improve their performance and increase their contribution to the change process. Leaders must also be mindful of their actions and behavior, as their actions can have a significant impact on the work environment and employee morale.

10. Continuously evaluate and adjust the approach

Leading change is not a one-time process, and leaders must continually evaluate and adjust their approach as needed. This requires being proactive and anticipating potential challenges, as well as being flexible and adaptable to the changes that may arise. Regular evaluations help ensure that the change process remains on track and that any issues are addressed quickly and effectively. Leaders must also be open to feedback and willing to modify their approach as necessary to ensure that the desired outcomes are achieved.

In conclusion, leading change effectively is an essential part of leadership in the business world. The ability to successfully implement change can have a significant impact on a company's success and growth. The strategies outlined above can help leaders lead change effectively, ensuring that the desired outcomes are achieved and that the process is as smooth as possible. However, leading change is not a one-time process, and leaders must continually evaluate and adjust their approach as needed. By being flexible, adaptable, and proactive, leaders can effectively lead change and position their companies for continued growth and success.

Leaders must also be mindful of the impact that change can have on employees and take steps to mitigate any negative effects. This may include providing support and resources and addressing any concerns or issues that employees may have. By being empathetic and understanding, leaders can help employees navigate the change process and emerge stronger on the other side.

In today's rapidly evolving business environment, leading change effectively is a crucial component of leadership. By following the strategies outlined above, leaders can lead change effectively and position their companies for continued growth and success. The ability to lead change effectively requires a combination of vision, communication, and leadership skills and is an essential component of success in the business world.

THE POWER OF POSITIVE CHANGE: CHARMEACHEALLE MOORE II AND WE L;VING

CHARMEACHEALLE MOORE II

We L;ving Inc. helps individuals become the most excellent version of themselves; by providing the resources and avenues for them to achieve greatness.

Hosea 4:6 states, "My people are destroyed for the lack of knowledge." Our platform provides the knowledge, inspiration, and village to help individuals reach their goals and discover their purpose in life.

We L;ving supports a diverse group of individuals, ranging from former professional athletes to those within the school system and their families.

The first group we focus on is athletes in transition. Growing up, my father always told me that if I made it to the NFL, all my dreams would come true. However, in my neighborhood during the 1990s and 2000s, we didn't have many role models for different career fields. Everyone just worked a regular job. This is where my company comes in. We understand the challenges athletes face during their transition period, whether it's from high school to college or from the NFL to life after the game.

We help bridge the gap and provide guidance for these individuals during this uncertain time. We also work to provide a positive impact in the communities where they live and stay, acting as a voice for both students and parents and supporting the school systems and community as a whole.

The second group we cater to is those in the school system. My experience as a long-term substitute teacher at Lakeview Centennial High School gave me valuable insight into the needs and challenges faced by schools today.

At We L;ving, we understand the importance of providing resources and opportunities to schools. But we also know that having a positive presence on campus can make a huge difference. That's why we bring in professional athletes to act as positive role models for students. They can assist with parental and community liaison and help with the

ABC model, which focuses on attendance, behavior, and academic success.

We believe that having professional athletes on campus can change the trajectory of a school for the better. They can provide a positive reinforcement that can help students succeed in school and in life. This is what we bring to the school system, and we are proud of it.

We understand schools are always looking for ways to increase parental involvement. That's why we offer parent clubs to bring families into the fold and give them the support they need. This ties into our third group of customers—parents. We believe that parenting is a team effort, and we want to be a village for parents to rely on.

Being a parent myself, I know how challenging it can be to balance providing for your family and being there for your child. Our parent clubs provide a space for parents to not only work on their relationship with their child but also to work on themselves. We want to help parents become the best version of themselves.

Another benefit of our parent clubs is that they help break down the barriers that can occur when a student is in school all day, receiving mentorship and support, but then goes back to the same environment at home. This can undo all the progress made at school and make it difficult to move forward. Our parent clubs help eliminate this reset and provide continuity for the child and family.

We understand that many of our clients are struggling with a sense of purpose and direction. They may feel stuck in a stagnant state and uncertain of how to move forward. This is where we come in.

Our goal is to provide a system and solution that will help our clients discover their true selves. We believe that self-discovery is key to finding one's purpose in life. We don't tell our clients who they should be or what they should do; instead, we empower them to identify their passions and strengths.

We L;ving is built on the principle of building people up. We believe in the importance of soft skills, such as communication, and we teach our clients how to identify the system they want to be successful in, whether it's the healthcare system, the NFL, teaching, or parenting. We want our clients to understand the ins and outs of the system they choose and to feel comfortable in it. We believe that by helping individuals find their true selves and understand the systems they want to be a part of, they can achieve success in any area they desire.

Many former professional athletes struggle to find their next step after their careers end. They've been so focused on their game for most of their lives that they don't know who they are without it. This can be a difficult and confusing time for them as they try to figure out what to do next.

Schools are also working on ways to capture the attention of their students and give them the information they need to succeed. They're also trying to get more parental involvement on campus to minimize drama and create a more positive environment for students and the community.

While the challenges faced by former athletes and schools may seem different on the surface, they both share a common goal: to help individuals and communities thrive. By working together and supporting each other, they can help create a brighter future for all involved.

From a parent's perspective, the school system is looking for help. Parents are often trying to understand and learn how to better themselves, while also creating a positive environment for their children. This is where organizations like We L;ving come in, by working with parents and children to help them achieve their goals.

A teacher can only teach what they know, but parents can also play an important role in guiding their children towards the right resources and opportunities. The pain and struggle that we work to ease is often centered on self-identity and understanding of what steps to take to provide for one's family and become a better person.

At We L;ving, we understand the importance of supporting parents and children in their journey towards self-discovery and personal growth. We strive to provide solutions and guidance to help ease the pain and struggles that so many families face. By working together, we can help create a brighter future for all involved.

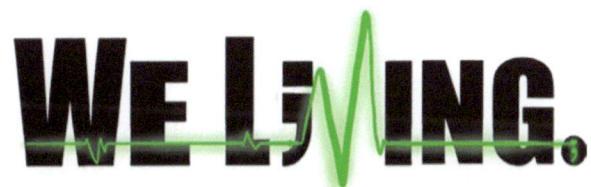

As professional athletes, parents, students, and school systems, we understand the importance of providing knowledge, wisdom, understanding, and know-how to help individuals achieve success. One of the key elements we focus on is the support effect, which helps to motivate individuals and carry them into their success.

One thing that we understand is that without knowledge, people can become destroyed. Hosea 4:6 states, "My people are destroyed for the lack of knowledge." This is something that we take seriously and strive to educate individuals on.

When I went into Lakeview Centennial High School, I had the mindset that students have the world in front of them and can achieve anything they want. However, many of my students would come to me and say, "Mr. Moore, how? I don't know anyone who is a doctor, lawyer, or in HVAC, or construction. How do I tap into this?" Despite coming to school every day, getting good grades, being on time, and having good behavior, these students had no interest in going to college and didn't know what they wanted to do.

It is our mission to provide the knowledge and support that will help individuals like these students tap into their potential and achieve success in their chosen field. We believe that with the right knowledge and support, anyone can achieve their dreams.

One of the key things we provide is knowledge. We believe that by providing knowledge and placing positive individuals in people's lives, we can help motivate, encourage, inspire, and support individuals in reaching their goals.

When I retired from the NFL, one of my mentors shared with me a valuable piece of advice: "Mike, if you want to be successful, find someone in that field who is successful. Take the great things they do and the bad things they do, mold that and turn that into your own, so you can come in and pick up off of what you learned from them."

We focus on placing positive individuals in the lives of students, parents, and professional athletes, as well as in the community. By providing an evolvable, sustainable, positive system of support to the community and school system, we aim to help motivate, mold, build, and structure positivity.

We also strive to bring in different job opportunities and industries and teach not only students but also parents and former professional athletes how to tap into those fields and understand that they can achieve their goals.

Our mission is to provide a village of support with different avenues and resources that promote success. We provide a voice for the voiceless and support individuals in reaching their full potential.

Our product offers the best solution for a custom approach to achieving success. We believe in a village mindset, where a group of individuals come together to support, motivate, encourage, and correct bad behaviors in order to help individuals reach their goals.

It doesn't matter if you're a former professional athlete, a parent, a student, a faculty member, or a school system in need of help. We provide a village of support that brings

in top-tier individuals to give knowledge, resources, and understanding of how to become successful in your chosen field. We cater to the specific needs of our clientele and help them find the field they find interesting.

Our approach is to provide an all-around support system that addresses the various needs of individuals and organizations. We believe that our product, Nonsense, is the perfect solution for anyone looking to improve and achieve success in their lives.

Our products and services are the best because we focus on people. We are a team of great individuals who are passionate about helping, working, motivating, and inspiring others. By starting with people and building them up, encouraging them, and providing them with the support they need, they can overcome any obstacles that come their way.

This is something that I've seen firsthand in the school system, as well as when working with former professional athletes. By having faith and trust in individuals and pointing them in the right direction to reach their desired goals or connecting them with people in their chosen field, we can help them achieve success.

That's why our product is the best solution. It offers not just a support base, but a support group that is led by individuals who have reached the highest level of success in their profession. We believe that this approach sets us apart and makes us the best in the business.

I started We L;ving out of personal experience. My journey began in 2019, when I retired from the NFL. The previous year, I had been waived from the team and found myself in a dark, hurt, and broken place. I

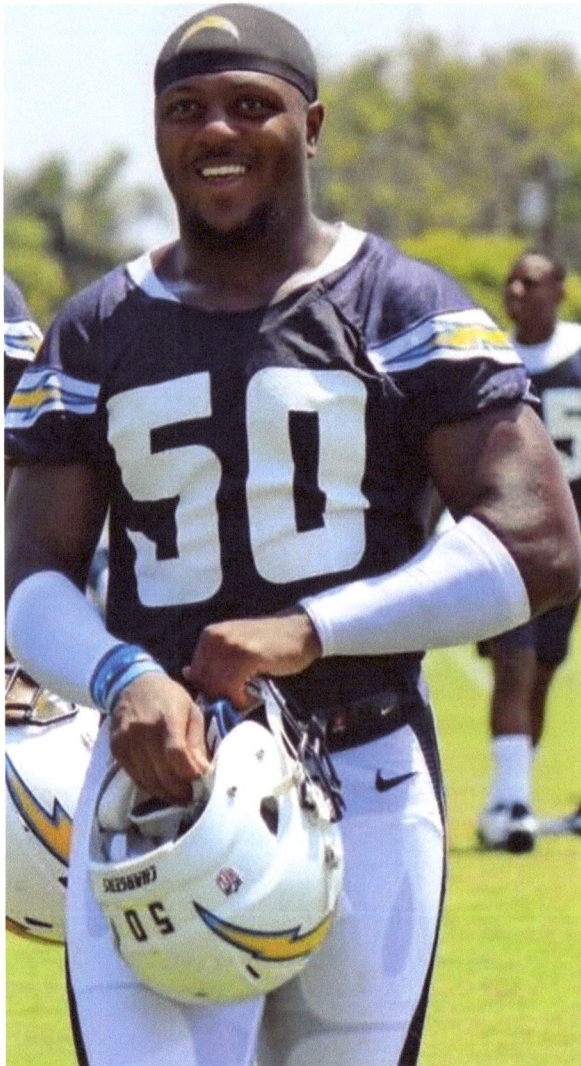

It was through these experiences that I realized the importance of support, motivation, and positivity in overcoming adversity. I started We L;ving to provide that support to others, to help them push through their struggles and reach their goals.

After I retired from the NFL, I faced the reality that the league didn't have a plan to take care of its players after their careers were over. The Hall of Fame players of the NFL proposed taking a pay cut to provide health insurance and a salary for just Hall of Fame players, and it was denied. This left many players, me included, feeling hurt and discarded. It was as if the league had used our bodies and then just thrown us away.

I faced a harsh reality that nobody had prepared me for. My mentor, a successful business executive, sat me down and said, "Mike, never say this to anybody else, but you can say this to me because of our relationship. The league didn't do you wrong. This is a business that you guys come into. They couldn't pay for your body. You had brain surgery in college. You had back surgery in the NFL. From a business standpoint, what would you pay for your body?"

was dealing with thoughts of suicide and was alone in California, divorced from my wife and separated from my children.

But I knew I had to keep going. I had already worked through so much, including brain surgery at Kansas State University in 2015, the death of my father, and a divorce while preparing for the NFL draft. And even after making it to the NFL, I was forced to retire due to brain surgery and back surgery.

It was at that moment that I realized the NFL was just a business, and that my body was a liability. Even though they tell you that NFL stands for Not For Long, I never thought it would happen to me. They only highlight the Emmett Smiths and Lawrence Taylors, the individuals who play eight to nine to ten to twelve years. But they don't highlight the individuals who only played one or two years, or the individuals who transition into something else after their career is over.

It wasn't until I had a conversation with the vice president of the NBA Players Association that I understood the importance of taking care of players after their careers were over. I was hurt and broken, but she made me realize that there was still a lot we could do to support and take care of former players.

And that's what led me to start We L;ving, to help players transition and support them after their careers are over. We believe that with the right knowledge and support, anyone can achieve their dreams.

When I realized that there was a gap in support for transitioning professional athletes, I knew I had found my niche. As the Vice President of the Dallas NFL Players Association, I met many former professional athletes from baseball, basketball, football, and the WNBA, and I saw a way for us to go into the school system and build up the entire community.

I saw an opportunity to bring resources to the school during the school day, where students spend 85% of their time. I saw the potential to put individuals on campus who have reached the highest point in their career and have shown success

Our goal is to bring different groups of individuals together and provide them with the knowledge and wisdom on how to get into a field and how to tap into a product. This can help boost a product, help people work for a company, and promote the product.

Building this company, We L;ving, has been a long journey, but it has been filled with success stories. We have helped many former professional athletes transition into a career field or land a job that they want. We have brought speakers into schools and hosted assemblies.

Skyline High School has been leading the way in social emotional learning (SEL) seminars for students in their district. Through the program, students have been able to learn from influential individuals who can help them from an emotional standpoint, as well as provide inspiration for different careers.

The program is built around the idea of helping students succeed by putting them in front of successful role models who are from similar backgrounds and to give them the tools to do the same.

Our first assembly was in May 2022, where 750 students participated, and the program has continued to grow. It has been a great success so far, and the team behind it is excited to continue to make a positive impact on the students in the district.

Are you looking for a way to make a positive impact in your community? Look no further than welving.org. Our organization is dedicated to helping individuals and groups reach their full potential.

If you're a professional athlete looking for support during the transition out of sports, we can help. We also work with athletes who have businesses or resources to share.

Parents, we understand the importance of having a supportive community. We can assist you in identifying goals and finding resources to help your children succeed.

School systems, we offer innovative solutions to capture students' attention and increase parental involvement on campus. Our sustainable and evolvable system can benefit not only students but also teachers and parents.

The best way to work with us is to reach out. Connect with us through our website, Instagram, Twitter, or LinkedIn. Contact our team through LinkedIn, and let's start a conversation about how we can bring our sustainable and evolvable system to your community.

When it comes to sharing the work of our organization, there's no substitute for personal experience. Whether it's through a conversation with me, being a part of one of our events, or talking to the people we've helped, the best way to truly understand what we do is to see it firsthand.

But for those who haven't had the chance to be directly involved, there are still plenty of ways to learn about and support our mission. Our website and social media channels are great resources to learn about our purpose and goals, and we encourage people to share those with their own networks.

Our organization is all about empowering individuals to move beyond a stagnant state and truly embrace life. We serve as a powerful voice for those who may have gone unheard, and we work to create a supportive community for everyone involved. This includes not just students, but parents, the school system, and even former professional athletes. Together, we're working to build up the community and make a real impact in the lives of those around us.

To be successful in life, there are three key things you must have: faith, patience, and the ability to discover resources.

Faith is crucial because it allows you to believe in yourself and know that you can achieve your goals. It doesn't matter if your goal is something as small as tying your shoe or something as big as getting a job or making it to the NFL, you must have faith that you will accomplish it. When you exercise faith, you understand nothing can deter you or stop you from reaching your goal and that God will give you the strength and courage to achieve it.

Patience is vital. It allows you to keep working towards your goal, perfecting yourself and knowing that it will happen. It means not giving up when things get tough and knowing that with time, hard work, and persistence, you will achieve your goal.

Having patience is a crucial skill for anyone looking to build something, whether it be a business, a career, or even a child. It takes time for any of these things to grow and develop, and without patience, it's easy to become discouraged or frustrated. It takes nine months for a baby to develop in a mother's womb. For a business, it can take three to five years before it becomes profitable.

And for some, it may take even longer to reach their goals. It took 20 years for me to get into the NFL, but I achieved my goal because I was patient. I kept working and operating in faith. I knew that even though the process was slow, I was still developing, cutting off things that didn't matter, and perfecting myself.

When the opportunity finally presented itself, I was ready. I was in the best shape possible to be successful. And that's why patience is key. When you're willing to put in the time and the work, you'll be ready when the time comes.

Finally, the ability to discover resources is essential. This means being able to find the people, tools, and information you need to help you achieve your goal. It's about having the drive and determination to find what you need to make your dream a reality.

Having the right resources is crucial for achieving success in life. No matter how intelligent or skilled you may be, without the resources, your goals will remain unfulfilled.

These resources can come in many forms, from the people you surround yourself with, to financial resources, to opportunities that present themselves. Recognizing and utilizing these resources is key to turning your vision into a reality.

It's important to operate in faith, knowing that the resources you need will come to you. This means actively working to perfect yourself and having the patience to wait for the right resources to present themselves.

When you have the right resources at your disposal, doors will open, and you will produce the things you want to create. Faith, patience, and resources are all crucial elements to achieving success.

By operating in faith, protecting and perfecting yourself, and having the patience to wait for the right opportunities, you can achieve your goals and walk into any room prepared and ready to succeed.

Learn more about We L;ving and Mike Moore at welving.org.

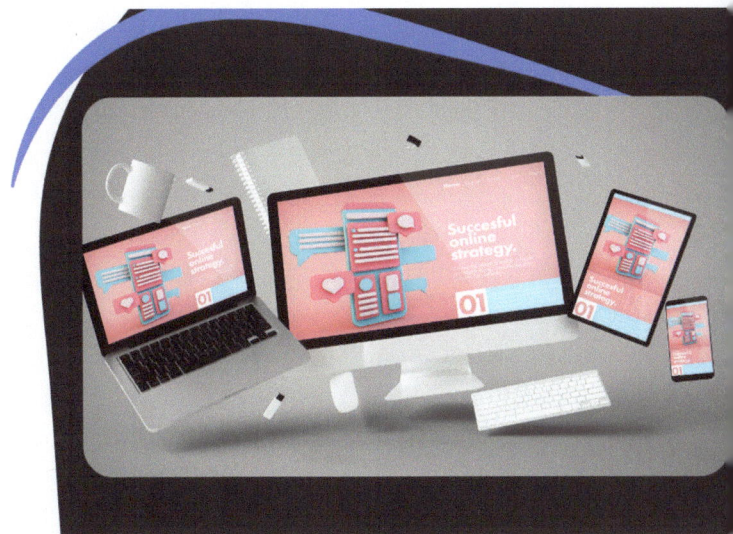

TRANSFORM THROUGH MENTORSHIP

LUBA SAKHARUK

I help women in technology to improve their skills and advance in their careers. I offer individual mentorship sessions and a cohort program where women can network and learn from other women in tech and me. The program includes online courses and guest speakers. I also work with decision-makers at companies, such as CTOs, to upskill their employees. My focus is on women in technology, but I work with anyone who is interested. My goal is to help women overcome any doubts they may have and achieve a fulfilling career, with a specific emphasis on developing skills that may be holding them back.

Many women in technology experience doubt about their abilities and feel unsure about taking on the next role. They may also struggle to present themselves as credible or confident in their skills and expertise. This is where I come in, as I offer mentorship and upskilling to help women overcome these doubts and improve their skills. On the other side, companies also have a need to upskill their employees and may not have the resources to do so internally. This is where I can help by offering my services to VPs of Engineering and Product to help them grow and manage their staff more effectively.

In 2023, I have four eight-week sessions planned that will help individuals become change architects and effective leaders. Each session includes an online course on Teachable that participants can complete at their own pace, as well as a weekly cohort group session with guest speakers. To further support their growth, participants will also have access to a one-on-one mentorship session to focus on specific areas they need to improve to advance in their careers.

I am an expert in the field of technology with a computer science degree and extensive experience in various roles. As a woman in tech, I understand the struggles and doubts that many face in the industry. To help others overcome these challenges, I offer a comprehensive program that caters to different learning styles. The program includes a self-paced course with videos, articles, and resources, as well as a weekly cohort group session with guest speakers and a one-on-one mentorship session. This ensures that people who prefer to learn independently have the resources to do so, while those who learn better in a group setting have the opportunity to ask questions, bounce ideas off of each other, and get support. Additionally, I provide offline support through text, Slack messages, and direct messaging. This is especially beneficial for those who may not feel comfortable speaking up in a group

or want extra support for a specific area, such as changing jobs or taking on a higher role. My program is designed to help women in tech increase their confidence and present themselves as experts in their fields.

I grew up in the former USSR, where soft skills were not highly valued, and I struggled with self-doubt due to my lack of proficiency in physics. Despite these obstacles, I went on to study computer science and earn a master's degree. I have extensive experience as a hands-on engineer, Scrum Master, Agile Coach, and consultant. Throughout my career, I have mentored and coached many women in the tech industry. Despite their intelligence and expertise, I have noticed that many of them have limiting beliefs and doubts that hold them back from reaching their full potential. They often don't entertain the idea of achieving more and immediately dismiss their own abilities. My passion is to mentor these women and help them overcome their doubts and achieve their goals.

Two years ago, my daughter was going through chemotherapy, and she told me that she was glad she was sick because it meant I could spend more time with her. This broke my heart and made me realize that I wanted more control over my schedule. I wanted the flexibility to build a business where I could make my own schedule and not have to travel all the time. So, in May 2021, I decided to start my own company, focusing on public speaking and facilitation. This way, I could schedule my work around my family's needs and have more control over my time.

In 2023, my focus will be on mentoring and upskilling women in technology. This is my passion and my purpose. Additionally, my goal is to create something scalable for my future so that I can have a fulfilling life and still be able to work. I don't want to feel useless after retirement, and I want to be able to do something that makes me feel valuable. While writing a memoir, I met a woman who wrote a book called *Becoming Retired(ish)*, and it made me realize that I want to create something that I can scale up or down depending on my needs and schedule. For example, if I want to travel once a month for a speaking engagement, I can do that. But if I need to earn more to support my children's education, I can do more speaking engagements or coaching sessions. My memoir is called *Life Worth Living*, and it reflects on the lessons I learned when my daughter was diagnosed with cancer. I want to inspire other women to question their limiting beliefs and see if there's more to their lives than what they're currently experiencing.

Recently, I worked with a woman who had been in the tech industry for a while but held a non-technical degree. She was doing the job of a very experienced Scrum Master but lacked the confidence to pursue the role further. The career path for a Scrum Master can lead to becoming an Agile Coach and various other roles. As an Agile Coach, it's all about facilitating sessions, training, and coaching people. But she didn't believe she was good enough for the role, even though I could see that she had the potential to excel in it. Through our coaching sessions, she was able to transfer into the role of a Scrum Master and got a $20,000 raise. She couldn't believe she deserved it, but with my support

and coaching, she gained confidence, and six months later, she landed an Agile Coach role at another company with a higher salary and more respect. This success story is a testament to the power of mentorship and coaching in helping individuals to recognize their potential and overcome their doubts and fears.

I have many stories like this of people who have overcome their doubts and fears through mentorship and coaching. One woman in particular had stayed home to raise her kids for six years and had a lot of technical knowledge and expertise but lacked confidence. Through our conversations, she realized that it wasn't other people who thought she had lost her skills but it was her own limiting beliefs. We agreed to work on positioning her as a thought leader and expert by recording podcasts and building her social presence. We also discussed how her skills as a mother and multitasker were transferable to the workforce and how she could leverage them to get back into the workforce. The change in her confidence level after just one conversation was very rewarding to see.

People can schedule a free consult with me at calendly.com/ralm3, or they can enroll in a program at ralm3.teachable.com. They can also check out my website for more info: www.ralm3.com.

The best way for someone to share about my services is to tell people they know directly. They can share information about my services on company forums and Slack channels, post links to my website and Teachable, and share my calendar link so people can schedule a time to talk with me.

If they know me personally and want to help, they can record a quick video message and post it on LinkedIn and tag me. There are many ways to help, and I don't have a preference as long as people know about the value I provide. If they know someone who could benefit from my services, that would be great. It could be a woman in tech or a leader who wants to bring me into their organization to create custom programs for them.

Doubts are a part of life, but we can choose how we react to them. We can either let them hold us back or use them as a tool to discover opportunities. If you're not happy with your current situation or want to explore what a life worth living could be, try looking at doubts as opportunities to take small actions. Identify the minimum steps you can take to move towards your goal. Don't settle for less than you deserve. Look into mentorship; it can help you transform doubts into opportunities and a life worth living.

WHAT NOBODY TOLD ME ABOUT BEING AN ENTREPRENEUR

SCOTT SERY

I accidentally became an entrepreneur. I didn't have a grand vision going into this thing. I didn't have this deep desire to give back, create jobs, or challenge myself to see if I could do it. No, this wasn't planned, and my career for the last tenish years has largely been an accident.

Rather than prepare for the entrepreneurial lifestyle, I had to learn all the things about being an entrepreneur after I had already started. But, by then, I was committed, and I just thought if I focused really hard and poured myself into this thing, it would all magically work out.

Things don't magically work out.

I have bumbled and scraped myself along over the years, but if I could go back in time and learn before jumping in, there are three things I wish the younger me had known.

1. Friends and family are not good clients

Hopefully, you have a good support network within your friends and family. And hopefully, they encourage you to pursue your dreams.

Maybe they will even buy from you if you're offering the right product or service that fits their needs. But by and large, they suck at being clients.

They suck for four reasons.

They want discounts. Listen, if you want to support a friend or family's business, that's great. However, if you go in asking for a friend and family discount, you might as well tell them that you don't value what they do. I will definitely give deals to people I like, but when a fledgling business is trying to make it, cheapening what they do is a surefire path to collapse.

They don't care about what you're doing. Your close friends and family likely don't care enough to go out of their way to understand what you're all about. In my writing business, I have friends I have known for over twenty years who still don't understand what I do—because they haven't taken the time to understand. It's not for lack of telling them, explicitly, everything I do; it's because it doesn't affect their life directly, and they don't really care.

They feel obligated to support you. You have a relationship, and they want to support you; the closer the relationship, the more support there is. Your immediate family will feel obligated to buy from you or hire you; that can strain the relationship if you're more expensive than what they're used to or you don't do as good of a job as those they usually buy from. Someone that buys from you because they think they have to won't become the raving fan you desire.

They give false hope. Everything else aside, the biggest reason they don't make good clients is that you're surrounded by "Yes Men." They are intent on not hurting your feelings, so they will give you praise when you need criticism, hope when you need to be put in your place, and instill the idea that you're going to become an overnight success when you likely won't even become a ten-year success. You need good, honest feedback, which rarely comes from people close to you.

2. You will suffer imposter syndrome forever

When I started, I didn't just jump into my business. I actually fell into it as I was working full-time as a financial advisor. (A job that I crashed and burned in; we'll talk about that in the next section.)

While freelancing here and there, writing magazine articles and blog posts to earn a little extra money, I would go through a range of emotions. First, I was excited that someone wanted to pay me for my work. Then I would fret about doing a great job because I wasn't sure what the heck I was doing. Then, after completing the work, I would have a handful of people read what I wrote because when I looked at it, I thought it absolutely sucked. After submitting it, I would get feedback on how to improve and sometimes a little praise on how nicely written it was.

The next gig I landed, I went through all those emotions again.

Over time, that imposter syndrome will start to wane. You'll feel like you're growing from the little fish in the little pond and becoming the big fish in the little pond. You know it when it hits, and eventually, you want out of that pond and into a bigger pond.

So, you expand your offering or raise your rates to attract better clients. And they will start to trickle on in. Then, suddenly, you're excited again, but now fretting if you know what the heck you're doing and biting your nails after you submit the work, wondering if they will hate your stuff. Perhaps you should discount the price, so they're not angry.

Imposter syndrome never goes away. It's going to cycle on through. Even if you know what you're doing and think you're hot stuff, you'll get that client that rips into you and complains about your incompetence.

As a writer, I get it. There have been numerous times when I would much rather flop onto the couch and scream into a pillow as I try to figure out what the heck I am doing. Yes, screaming into pillows is done at least a few times every week.

3. You need to learn how to fail

Living life as an entrepreneur, you will fail. You will fail a lot. That's nothing new; if you have read anything about running a

business or being an entrepreneur, you have probably heard this advice before.

Fail fast. Fail often. Fail forward. Fail fa-la la-la la-la. Eventually, it's just noise in the background.

But there's a whole lot more to failing than most people think. And failure comes in a whole bunch of flavors besides the obvious. The real trick is to learn how to fail so that you don't feel like you have failed. And that takes a lot of work.

When I worked as a financial advisor, I could close deals like no other. I had something like a 90%+ close rate—when I could get people in the door. But over time, I couldn't set appointments. I struggled to contact even a handful of people each day, and often I wasn't able to get them to meet with me. When I looked at my activity, I was doing everything I was taught to do but failed because I didn't change and figure out what

would work better. I didn't even last a year in that position.

Statistically speaking, most entrepreneurs won't last more than a few years. Then, as they close up shop, they can go through a whole host of reasons why they failed.

"The community didn't support me." Or "Covid caused delays." Or "It wasn't the right time." Or "The Lizard People are out to get me, man!"

They might all be valid reasons; I can't tell you how many times I have had to fight off the Lizard People as they try to plunge me into ruin. But often, there's a simpler reason the door was locked up for good: they didn't charge enough.

It might not seem like it, but charging too little is a failure. Even if your business pulls through, brings in enough money, and doesn't completely fold, undercharging

is almost as big a deal as overcharging. Here's why.

Most new entrepreneurs have spent years developing their skill sets. They have poured into it, studied, practiced, and honed their craft. Then, when it comes time to offer their service, they want to bring in as many clients as possible, so they price themselves too low. Unfortunately, doing so has a double-whammy effect on the business.

First, the clientele coming through the doors is of a lower caliber. They're the ones that will complain, beg, cause delays, and get mad. Those willing to pay a higher price know your value and are happy to pay it.

Second, you have a ton of work to do—and you're barely making ends meet. So now you're stressing because you have to get all this work done, you can't put the time into every project, and you're exhausted. Under-pricing doesn't help you, it doesn't help your clients, and overall, it's a means of failing.

Failure isn't just trying something and not succeeding. It can be an inability to close deals, maybe building a course that sucks and nobody buys (I'm guilty of that one—I don't know if it sucked, but nobody bought it), or it's just wasting time watching cat videos online when you should be thinking of ways that actually work instead of bemoaning the fact that you have no clients.

What I wish I had known before I started out as an entrepreneur, or at least at the beginning, entails a lot. Who wouldn't want to know everything they know now but years earlier?

However, learning how to spot failure and take steps to fix it would work wonders when it comes down to it. Knowing that you will always feel like you don't know what the heck you're doing is the only way to drive you to learn more and grow bigger. And then focus your marketing efforts outside your existing circle so that you don't waste your time with people who blow smoke up your you-know-where; that's when you're going to do better and succeed faster.

About the Author

Scott Sery ghost writes books and provides some of the best copywriting the world has ever seen. He recently turned 287 years old - older than most trees; he can hear your thoughts before you speak them.

MAXIMIZE YOUR MESSAGE WITH THE HELP OF AUDIVITA STUDIOS

DAVID WOLF

At Audivita Studios, our ideal client is the author, the speaker, the thought leader, the nonprofit, the corporation, and the company that wants to get its voice out into the world through podcasts or audiobooks. And we help them do just that.

The problems we solve for our clients are the mechanics, the technology, the timing, and the regularity of production. That's true on the podcast side of the equation. On the audiobook side of the equation, we help our clients find the perfect voice for their book and/or facilitate the recording of their own audiobook as an author and then get it out into the world. Many of our clients would be greatly challenged if they didn't have a partner like us to help them with all the technology, distribution, and production processes.

Our main products are podcasts and audiobooks. Those are the two types of communications we produce and deliver for our clients. We're finding more and more that we're helping our clients promote their work through social media marketing, now an additional service we offer.

We know that there are many ways to produce an audiobook or podcast and get it to market. We're in a highly competitive market. Why work with us? We're a high-touch, hands-on, and engaging solution. We aren't a gold, silver, and bronze package kind of company. We take a very customized approach to production, whether it's an audiobook or a podcast. We're part of your team, the author's team, the podcaster's team, and the company's team. People like to work with us for those reasons and others. And I think that's the most important quality we bring that sets us apart from some of our competitors.

I come from a music background. I was born and raised in Chicago and was involved in the commercial music scene, writing and producing music for radio, TV, film, commercials, and children's shows. When I turned forty, I ventured into other things and made a business turnaround. Sometime after that, I returned to my roots and created this team—a spectacular team. It was a happy coincidence. The right people got on the bus at the right time to start this company called Audivita Studios. It all started with me as a solopreneur. I produced my podcast, Small Business America, and got a few audiobook projects I recorded, edited, and produced myself. At a certain point, the scale of the business exceeded what I could handle on my own. So I systematically got

help, and that's actually how we came to be. Today, our management team comprises four people plus me—we call ourselves the Fab Five—and about two dozen freelancers, mostly in North America and some countries overseas. And we continue to grow.

One of our success stories is a project we're working on right now. My friends Anthony Marinelli and Steven Ray worked with Michael Jackson and Quincy Jones forty years ago on the best-selling album of all time called *Thriller*. They came to me and said, "We want to take the stories from this room out into the world." The stories of the musicians, the singers, the musicians, the creative nuances, and the experiences they had making this album with Michael and Quincy. They didn't really know how to go about it. So we started producing a series of video and audio podcasts for them to get those stories out into the world. Today, we're reaching millions of people through Instagram, Facebook, YouTube, and all the popular podcast channels to spread this story. It's a happy ending, and it continues.

The best way for an author, speaker, thought leader or aspiring podcaster, or a company that wants to podcast, to work with us starts with a call to me or one of our other senior team members. I usually have an initial conversation to get a feel for you, your project, and your ideas. If you're not sure what you have in mind yet, our process helps you better define what you want to say and how you want to get your voice out into the world through this medium. It's a very interactive and collaborative process that starts with a phone call to us. You can email me at dwolf@audivita.com.

A lot of our business comes from word of mouth. We have many satisfied authors and podcasters, so the business has grown rather organically over the last four years since we started. We have a website, Audivita.com, which has many pages with examples of our work and testimonials. There's a team page where you can get a sense of who's behind the company, which we think is very important. We have a very high-quality team. That's an important part of our message and sets us apart from the competition. Sharing the work we do through our website or just giving a referral is a wonderful way to share the work we do here.

I think we're all in the media business today thanks to social media and the ability to easily record, edit and produce content. And the way we put our voice out into the world is through content. Even if you're an introvert, getting your voice out into the world and communicating and connecting is an important part of your job.

We encourage you to at least try producing a podcast series or appearing on other people's podcasts. And if you're a writer, taking part in the audio market has become essential. That market has grown by 28% every year since 2015. It's still an exploding market. We believe that participating in this market is extremely important for anyone who wants to get their voice out into the world.

About the Author

David Wolf, Music Composer/Producer turned media entrepreneur founded Audivita Studios in 2017 to help authors, speakers, businesses, and thought leaders connect their voices to the world with audiobooks and original podcasts. Today his team produces and distributes 50 original podcasts and 200 audiobooks annually.

SMART BUSINESS GROWTH: A STEP-BY-STEP GUIDE

Growing a business can be a challenging and complex journey. It requires strategic planning, careful execution, and a willingness to adapt and evolve as the market changes. But with the right approach, it can also be incredibly rewarding. In this blog post, we will take you through a step-by-step guide to smart business growth. We cover the essential elements that will help you take your business to the next level, including understanding your business, optimizing operations, and adapting to change. Whether you're a startup just starting out or a seasoned business owner looking to scale, you'll receive practical insights and actionable tips to help you reach your growth goals. So let's get started on the journey toward smart business growth.

Understanding Your Business

The first step towards smart business growth is understanding your business. This requires a deep dive into the strengths and weaknesses of your business, as well as an understanding of your target audience and the market you operate in. With this knowledge in hand, you will make informed decisions that will help drive growth. In this section, we will explore the key elements of understanding your business, including market research and analysis, defining your business goals, and understanding your target audience.

Market Research and Analysis

Market research and analysis is gathering and analyzing information about your industry, your competitors, and your target audience. This information will help you better understand the market you operate in and provide you with valuable insights into how to position your business for growth. To conduct market research and analysis, you can use a variety of tools, including online surveys, focus groups, and competitor analysis. You can also attend industry events and conferences and speak to experts in your field.

Defining Your Business Goals

Once you have a good understanding of your market, it's time to turn your attention to defining your business goals. This will involve setting clear, measurable objectives that will guide your decision-making and inform your growth strategy. When setting your business goals, it's important to be realistic and consider the resources you have available to you. It's also important to align your goals with your business values and mission so that you stay true to what your business is all about.

Understanding Your Target Audience

Finally, it's important to have a deep understanding of your target audience. This includes knowing who they are, what their needs and wants are, and how they prefer to be engaged. You can use a variety of tools, including surveys, customer feedback, and social media analytics, to get a better understanding of your target audience. By understanding your target audience, you will tailor your marketing and sales efforts and create products and services that meet their needs.

Understanding your business is a critical first step toward smart growth. By taking the time to conduct market research and analysis, define your business goals, and understand your target audience, you will make informed decisions that will drive growth and position your business for success. Stay tuned for the next section, where we explore the importance of a strong marketing strategy.

Marketing Strategy

A strong marketing strategy is essential for any business looking to grow. It's creating awareness of your brand, building relationships with customers, and driving sales. In this section, we will explore the key elements of a successful marketing strategy, including identifying your unique value proposition, building a strong brand, using digital marketing, and networking and building relationships with other businesses.

Identifying Your Unique Value Proposition

Your unique value proposition (UVP) is what sets your business apart from your competitors. It's the reason customers should choose your business over any other. To identify your UVP, you need to understand what your customers want and what makes your business unique. This could be a combination of your products, services, customer experience, or any other factor that differentiates you from the competition. Once you have identified your UVP, you can use it to guide your marketing and sales efforts and communicate it clearly to your target audience.

Building a Strong Brand

A strong brand is a key driver of business growth. It helps build awareness of your business, creates customer loyalty, and positions you as a leader in your industry. To build a strong brand, you need to clearly understand your business values and mission and communicate it consistently through all your marketing efforts. This could include creating a strong brand identity, using consistent messaging, and

engaging with customers through social media and other channels.

Utilizing Digital Marketing

In today's digital age, utilizing digital marketing is essential for any business looking to grow. Digital marketing includes a range of online and offline marketing efforts, including search engine optimization (SEO), pay-per-click advertising (PPC), email marketing, social media marketing, and more. By utilizing digital marketing, you can reach a wider audience, build brand awareness, and drive sales. To be successful with digital marketing, it's important to deeply understand your target audience, create compelling content, and use data-driven insights to make informed decisions.

Networking and Building Relationships with Other Businesses

Networking and building relationships with other businesses is a key part of any marketing strategy. This can help you reach new customers, learn from other business owners, and create partnerships that drive growth. Networking can take many forms, such as attending industry events and conferences, taking part in local business groups, and forming strategic alliances with other businesses. By building relationships with other businesses, you can create new opportunities for growth and position your business for success.

Financial Planning: Building a Strong Financial Foundation

Financial planning is a crucial aspect of business growth. It involves developing a comprehensive plan for managing your finances, including setting financial goals, forecasting revenue and expenses, and tracking your progress. In this section, we will explore the key elements of effective financial planning, including setting financial goals, creating a budget, managing cash flow, and seeking professional advice.

Setting Financial Goals

Setting financial goals is an essential first step in effective financial planning. This involves defining what you want to achieve financially and how you plan to get there. Your financial goals should be specific, measurable, and aligned with your overall business strategy. Some common financial goals for businesses include increasing revenue, reducing costs, improving profitability, and building a cash reserve.

Creating a Budget

A budget is a critical tool for managing your finances and ensuring that your business remains on track. A budget helps you track your income and expenses and provides a roadmap for achieving your financial goals. To create an effective budget, you need to clearly understand your business's revenue and expenses and regularly update it to reflect changes in your financial situation.

Managing Cash Flow

Cash flow is the movement of money in and out of your business. Effective cash flow management is critical for business growth, as it helps ensure that you have sufficient funds to cover your expenses, pay bills on time, and invest in growth opportunities. To manage cash flow effectively, you need to stay aware of your income and expenses, regularly track your cash balance, and implement strategies for managing fluctuations in cash flow.

Seeking Professional Advice

Seeking professional advice is an important part of effective financial planning. A financial advisor or accountant can help you develop a comprehensive financial plan, manage your finances, and make informed decisions about your business. They can also provide valuable insights and expertise and help you navigate the complexities of financial regulations and compliance.

Operations Optimization: Streamlining Your Business Processes

Operations optimization is streamlining and improving your business processes to increase efficiency, reduce costs, and improve customer satisfaction. In this section, we will explore the key elements of effective operations optimization, including process mapping, standardization, automation, and continuous improvement.

Process Mapping

Process mapping is a visual representation of the steps involved in a particular business process. By mapping out your processes, you can gain a clear understanding of how workflows through your organization, identify inefficiencies, and develop strategies for improvement. There are various tools and techniques for process mapping, including flowcharts, swimlane diagrams, and value stream maps.

Standardization

Standardization involves establishing consistent processes and procedures across your organization. By standardizing your processes, you can reduce errors, improve quality, and increase efficiency. Standardization also makes it easier to train new employees and scale your business as you grow.

Automation

Automation involves using technology to automate repetitive tasks and processes. Automation can help reduce errors, improve efficiency, and increase productivity. Automated processes are also faster, more consistent, and more reliable than manual processes. When selecting automation tools, it is important to choose ones that integrate with your existing systems and meet the specific needs of your business.

Continuous Improvement

Continuous improvement is a mindset that emphasizes continuous improvement and innovation. By regularly reviewing and updating your processes, you can identify areas for improvement, make changes, and continuously optimize your operations. Continuous improvement helps ensure that your business stays competitive and adapts to changing market conditions.

Adapting to Change: Staying Ahead of the Curve

Change is inevitable, and businesses must adapt to survive and grow. In this section, we explore the importance of being flexible and agile in the face of change and discuss strategies for staying ahead of the curve.

Embracing Change

Embracing change is critical for business growth. By being open to new ideas and embracing change, you can stay ahead of the curve and continuously improve your business. This requires a willingness to take risks, try new things, and experiment with new strategies and approaches.

Staying Up to Date

Staying up to date with the latest trends and developments in your industry is important for staying ahead of the curve. This requires continuous learning and education, attending conferences and events, and following industry experts and thought leaders.

Being Flexible

Being flexible and agile is essential for adapting to change. By having the ability to pivot quickly, you can respond to changing market conditions and stay ahead of the curve. This requires having a flexible business model, a willingness to adapt, and the ability to quickly make changes when necessary.

Collaborating with Others

Collaborating with others—such as partners, suppliers, and customers—can help you stay ahead of the curve. By working together, you can share ideas, knowledge, and resources and develop innovative solutions to meet changing market conditions.

Adapting to change is critical for business growth. By embracing change, staying up to date, being flexible, and collaborating with others, you can stay ahead of the curve and continuously improve your business. In today's rapidly changing business environment, the ability to adapt and respond to change is essential for success.

In conclusion, business growth requires a combination of strategy, planning, and execution. This includes understanding your business, having a marketing strategy, a financial plan, optimized operations, and exceptional customer service. Continuously assess progress, set goals, track progress, and seek professional advice to ensure success. Business growth is a journey, and by taking a step-by-step approach, you can build a sustainable business that achieves its full potential.

FROM START-UP TO SCALE-UP

Starting a business is a significant accomplishment, but it's only the first step in a long journey. The next challenge is to scale the business, take it to the next level and reach its full potential. The transition from a start-up to a scale-up can be challenging, but with the right strategy, preparation, and execution, it's possible to achieve success. In this blog post, we will delve into the key elements of transitioning from a start-up to a scale-up, including understanding the differences between the two, preparation, overcoming common challenges, and best practices for success. Whether you're just starting out or you're looking to take your business to the next level, this guide is a must-read for entrepreneurs.

Understanding the difference between Start-up and Scale-up

Understanding the difference between a start-up and a scale-up is essential to successfully transitioning your business. While the two terms are often used interchangeably, they have distinct characteristics that set them apart. In this section, we will take a

closer look at the key differences between a start-up and a scale-up.

A start-up is a new business venture that is focused on finding a product/market fit and growing as quickly as possible. Start-ups are often characterized by their entrepreneurial mindset, limited resources, and a focus on innovation. Entrepreneurs who start businesses with a start-up mindset are typically more risk-tolerant and willing to try new and unconventional approaches. This mindset is necessary to get the business off the ground, but it's not always the best approach for long-term success.

On the other hand, a scale-up is a business that has found its product/market fit and is now focused on growing as efficiently and sustainably as possible. Scale-ups have a more structured approach to growth, a focus on scalability, and a willingness to invest in resources and infrastructure. These investments are critical to scaling the business and achieving long-term success.

One of the key differences between a start-up and a scale-up is their focus. A start-up is primarily focused on finding a product/market fit, while a scale-up is focused on growing and scaling the business. This shift in focus requires a change in mindset, strategy, and execution. A start-up may be willing to take risks and try new and unconventional approaches, while a scale-up is more focused on refining processes, optimizing performance, and building a sustainable business model.

Another key difference is the approach to growth. Start-ups often focus on growth at all costs, while scale-ups are more focused on profitable growth. This means that scale-ups are more willing to make the necessary investments in resources and infrastructure to achieve sustainable growth, while start-ups may be more focused on cutting costs to reach profitability.

Understanding the differences between a start-up and a scale-up is critical to successfully transitioning your business. While the two terms are often used interchangeably, they have distinct characteristics that set them apart. By understanding these differences, you can make informed decisions about your business and set yourself up for long-term success.

Preparation for the transition

Preparation is key to successfully transitioning from a start-up to a scale-up. The transition can be challenging, but with the right preparation, you can set your business up for long-term success. In this section, we will take a closer look at what it takes to prepare for the transition from a start-up to a scale-up.

1. **Assess Your Business:** The first step in preparing for the transition is to assess your business. This includes conducting a thorough analysis of your market, customers, competition, and internal operations. This will give you a clear understanding of your strengths and weaknesses and help you identify areas that need improvement.

2. **Refine Your Business Model:** Based on your assessment, it's time to refine your business model. This may involve making changes to your products, services, or processes. The goal is to ensure that your business model is scalable and sustainable in the long term.

3. **Build Strong Relationships:** Strong relationships with customers, suppliers, and partners are critical to scaling your business. As you prepare for the transition, take the time to build strong, lasting relationships with these key stakeholders.

4. **Hire the Right Team:** As your business grows, you will need to hire additional staff. It's important to hire the right people for the right roles and to build a team that is aligned with your company's values and mission.

5. **Plan for Growth:** To ensure a successful transition, you need to have a clear plan for growth. This should include projections for revenue, expenses, and staffing, as well as a timeline for reaching your goals.

6. **Invest in Resources and Infrastructure:** Scaling a business requires investment in resources and infrastructure. This may include investments in technology, marketing, and sales, as well as the physical infrastructure required to support growth.

7. **Continuously Monitor and Adjust:** The transition from a start-up to a scale-up is not a one-time event. It's a continuous process that requires ongoing monitoring and adjustment. Be prepared to continuously assess your business, make changes as needed, and adapt to the evolving market.

Preparation is key to successfully transitioning from a start-up to a scale-up. By conducting a thorough assessment, refining your business model, building strong relationships, hiring the right team, planning for growth, investing in resources and infrastructure, and continuously monitoring and adjusting, you can set your business up for long-term success.

Overcoming common challenges during the transition

The transition from a start-up to a scale-up is not without its challenges. As your business grows, you will face new and unique challenges that require a different set of skills and strategies to overcome. In this section, we will take a closer look at some of the common challenges you may face during the transition and how to overcome them.

1. **Managing Growth:** One of the biggest challenges of scaling a business is managing growth. As your business grows, you need to have the right systems, processes, and people in place to support that growth. This can be a complex and time-consuming process, but it's essential for long-term success.

2. **Maintaining Culture:** As you hire new employees and expand your operations, it's important to maintain the culture and values that made your business successful in the first place. This can be challenging, but it's essential to preserving the unique identity of your business.

3. **Balancing Costs and Investments:** As you scale your business, you need to balance the need for investments with the need to control costs. This can be a delicate balancing act, but it's essential to achieving long-term success.

4. **Adapting to Market Changes:** The market is constantly evolving, and it's important to be able to adapt to these changes. This requires being flexible and open to change and being able to pivot quickly when necessary.

5. **Building Strong Relationships:** As your business grows, it's important to build strong relationships with customers, suppliers, and partners. This requires taking the time to understand their needs and working collaboratively to find mutually beneficial solutions.

6. **Maintaining Product Quality:** As you scale your business, it's important to

maintain the quality of your products and services. This requires investing in quality control systems and processes and continuously monitoring and improving quality.

7. **Managing Risk:** Scaling a business involves taking risks, and it's important to manage these risks effectively. This requires having a clear understanding of the risks involved and taking steps to minimize them.

The transition from a start-up to a scale-up is not without its challenges. By understanding and overcoming these challenges, you can set your business up for long-term success. Whether it's managing growth, maintaining culture, balancing costs and investments, adapting to market changes, building strong relationships, maintaining product quality, or managing risk, the key to success is preparation, persistence, and a willingness to learn and adapt.

Best practices for successful scale-up

The transition from a start-up to a scale-up can be a complex and challenging process, but with the right approach, it can be a rewarding experience that sets your business up for long-term success. In this section, we will explore some of the best practices for a successful scale-up.

1. **Develop a Strong Strategy:** A strong strategy is the foundation for any successful scale-up. This requires defining your goals, understanding your customers, and developing a plan for growth. It's important to regularly review and adjust your strategy as needed to ensure it continues to align with your business goals.

2. **Focus on Customer Experience:** Customer experience is the key to long-term success, and it's important to focus on it as you scale your business. This requires understanding your customers, their needs, and what they value. It also requires investing in systems and processes to improve the customer experience and continuously monitoring and refining it.

3. **Build a Strong Team:** A strong team is the backbone of any successful business. As you scale your business, it's important to build a team of talented, dedicated, and motivated employees who are committed to your success. This requires investing in employee development, creating a positive workplace culture, and fostering collaboration and teamwork.

4. **Invest in Technology:** Technology can play a critical role in the success of your scale-up. Whether it's automating processes, improving efficiency, or enhancing the customer experience, technology can help you overcome many of the challenges you will face as you scale your business.

5. **Focus on Continuous Improvement:** Continuous improvement is the key to staying ahead of the competition and achieving long-term success. This requires regularly reviewing and refining your systems, processes, and products to ensure they continue to meet the changing needs of your customers and the market.

6. **Manage Cash Flow Effectively:** Effective cash flow management is essential to the success of your scale-up. This requires monitoring and managing expenses, optimizing pricing, and improving collections processes.

7. **Foster a Culture of Innovation:** Innovation is the key to staying ahead of the competition and finding new and better ways to serve your customers. This requires fostering a culture of innovation that encourages creativity, experimentation, and risk-taking.

In conclusion, the transition from a start-up to a scale-up can be a complex and challenging process, but with the right approach, it can be a rewarding experience that sets your business up for long-term success. Whether it's developing a strong strategy, focusing on customer experience, building a strong team, investing in technology, focusing on continuous improvement, managing cash flow effectively, or fostering a culture of innovation, the key to success is preparation, persistence, and a willingness to learn and adapt.

DOING GOOD IS
GOOD BUSINESS

SHARING THE CREDIT

THE FUTURE OF BUSINESS GROWTH: PREDICTIONS AND STRATEGIES

The world of business is constantly evolving, and staying ahead of the curve is essential for success. As technology advances and consumer demands change, businesses must adapt and grow in order to remain competitive. The future of business growth is uncertain, but by looking at trends and considering expert predictions, we can gain valuable insights into what lies ahead. In this blog post, we'll examine some of the most promising predictions for the future of business growth, as well as strategies for businesses to stay ahead of the game. Whether you're a seasoned entrepreneur or just starting out, this post is a must-read for anyone looking to grow their business in the coming years.

Predictions for the Future of Business Growth

The future of business is uncertain, but by examining current trends and considering expert predictions, we can gain valuable insights into what the future may hold. In this section, we'll take a closer look at some of the most promising predictions for the future of business growth. These predictions are based on the current state of the market, as well as emerging trends in technology, consumer behavior, and business practices. Whether you're a seasoned entrepreneur or just starting out, these predictions can help you plan for the future and make informed decisions about the direction of your business.

Increased Emphasis on Digital Transformation

In today's digital age, technology is playing an increasingly important role in business success. From automation to artificial intelligence, the use of technology is becoming more and more integrated into the fabric of modern business practices. In the future, we can expect to see an even greater emphasis on digital transformation as businesses look to stay ahead of the curve and stay competitive.

One of the biggest drivers of this trend is the importance of technology in the modern business landscape. As technology continues to evolve, businesses must be able to keep up with the latest advancements in order to remain relevant. For example, the rise of automation and artificial intelligence is changing the way that businesses operate, streamlining processes and reducing costs. In the future, businesses that are able to leverage these technologies to their advantage will be better positioned for success.

Another important aspect of digital transformation is the adoption of remote work. In recent years, the COVID-19 pandemic has accelerated the trend of remote work, and it's likely that this trend will continue in the future. This means that businesses must be able to adapt to a more distributed workforce and ensure that their employees have the tools and technology they need to work effectively from anywhere. Whether it's through cloud computing, collaboration tools, or virtual meetings, businesses must embrace digital transformation in order to stay competitive in the future.

Importance of Customer Experience

Another key trend that's shaping the future of business growth is the importance of customer experience. As consumers become increasingly demanding, businesses must focus on delivering a top-notch customer experience in order to remain competitive. This means understanding the needs and expectations of your customers and developing strategies to meet those needs in a personalized and meaningful way.

One of the biggest drivers of this trend is the need to meet customer expectations. Consumers today have access to a wealth of information and are more informed than ever before. They know what they want, and they expect businesses to deliver on those expectations. Whether it's fast shipping, personalized recommendations, or a seamless online shopping experience, businesses must be able to deliver the customer experience that their customers demand.

Another important aspect of customer experience is building customer loyalty. In today's competitive landscape, customer loyalty is more important than ever. By delivering a great customer experience, businesses can build strong, long-lasting relationships with their customers, which can lead to increased customer loyalty and repeat business. Whether it's through customer service, personalization, or other customer-focused strategies, businesses must focus on delivering a top-notch customer experience in order to thrive in the future.

The Rise of Sustainable Business Models

In recent years, there has been a growing emphasis on sustainability and corporate social responsibility. Consumers are becoming more environmentally conscious, and they expect businesses to do their part in protecting the planet. As a result, sustainable business models are becoming increasingly popular, and we can expect to see this trend continue in the future.

One of the biggest drivers of this trend is the growing number of environmentally conscious consumers. People today are more aware of the impact of their consumption habits on the environment, and they are looking for companies that share their values. By adopting sustainable practices, businesses can not only reduce their environmental impact but can also differentiate themselves from their competitors and build a strong reputation with consumers.

Another important aspect of sustainable business models is the cost savings associated with being more environmentally friendly. For example, reducing energy use through the implementation of energy-efficient technology can help businesses reduce their operating costs while also reducing their carbon footprint. Similarly, reducing waste through the implementation of recycling and composting programs can also help businesses save money in the long run.

In addition to these benefits, sustainable business models can also help businesses stay ahead of the curve. As environmental regulations become increasingly strict, businesses that are proactive in their approach to sustainability will be better positioned to comply with these regulations and avoid potential fines or penalties.

Strategies for Business Growth

In today's highly competitive business landscape, companies need to constantly evaluate and adapt their strategies in order to drive growth and remain relevant. With rapidly changing market conditions and advancements in technology, it's essential for businesses to have a roadmap for success. In this section, we will explore some of the key strategies that businesses can implement in order to achieve growth in the future.

Invest in Technology

Technology continues to play an increasingly important role in business success, making it essential for companies to invest in the tools and technologies they need to remain competitive. Whether it's through automation, artificial intelligence, or other technological advancements, investing in technology can help businesses streamline their operations, reduce costs, and increase efficiency.

For example, implementing automation technologies can help businesses automate repetitive tasks, freeing up valuable resources to focus on more strategic initiatives. Additionally, the use of artificial intelligence can help businesses optimize their operations, making better use of data to drive decision-making and drive growth.

Prioritize Customer Experience

In today's customer-centric marketplace, delivering a top-notch customer experience is more important than ever. Companies that are able to build strong relationships with their customers are more likely to drive growth and succeed in the long term. To achieve this, businesses need to prioritize the customer experience at every touchpoint, from the initial point of sale to post-purchase follow-up.

This may include developing personalized marketing campaigns, investing in customer service technologies, and using customer feedback to continuously improve the overall experience. By understanding the needs and expectations of their customers, companies can develop strategies that meet those needs in a meaningful and relevant way, leading to increased customer loyalty and advocacy.

Adopt Sustainable Practices

Consumers are becoming increasingly aware of the impact their consumption habits have on the environment, and they are looking for companies that share their values. Adopting sustainable practices can help businesses reduce their environmental impact set position themselves above their competitors and build a strong reputation with consumers.

From reducing energy use through energy-efficient technology to implementing recycling and composting programs, businesses can reduce waste and operating costs while also aligning with consumer values. By being proactive in their approach to sustainability, companies can also stay ahead of the curve as environmental regulations become increasingly strict.

Diversify Revenue Streams

In today's fast-paced business environment, companies need to be agile and flexible in order to stay ahead of the curve. Diversifying revenue streams can help businesses reduce their dependence on a single source of income, providing a safety net in the event of market fluctuations.

This may involve expanding into new product lines or markets, developing partnerships with other businesses, or exploring alternative revenue streams such as subscriptions, advertising, or licensing. By having a diverse portfolio of revenue streams, businesses can weather market fluctuations and continue to drive growth in the long term.

Foster a Culture of Innovation

Innovation is a key driver of business growth, and companies that foster a culture of innovation are more likely to succeed in the long term. This means encouraging creativity, taking calculated risks, and investing in research and development.

Businesses can achieve this by developing processes that encourage idea generation and experimentation, providing resources for new projects and initiatives, and recognizing and rewarding innovative thinking. By fostering a culture of innovation, companies can stay ahead of the curve, remain relevant in the market, and continue to drive growth in the years to come.

In conclusion, the future of business growth is driven by a combination of technology, customer experience, sustainability, diversified revenue streams, and a culture of innovation. By implementing these strategies, companies can build a roadmap.

Importance of Data and Analytics for Business Growth

In the modern business landscape, data and analytics play a critical role in driving growth and success. By harnessing the power of data and analytics, companies can make informed decisions, improve their operations, and gain a competitive edge. In this section, we'll explore the importance of data and analytics for business growth and how companies can harness this valuable resource.

Better Decision Making

One of the primary benefits of data and analytics is the ability to make better, more informed decisions. By analyzing data, businesses can gain insights into key performance metrics, customer behavior, and market trends, enabling them to make decisions based on real-world evidence. This leads to improved decision-making and increased efficiency, which can drive business growth and success.

Improved Customer Understanding

Data and analytics can also help companies better understand their customers, including their needs, preferences, and behaviors. By analyzing customer data, companies can develop more targeted and personalized marketing strategies, leading to increased customer engagement and sales. Additionally, businesses can use customer data to identify trends and patterns in customer behavior, helping them stay ahead of the curve and respond to changing market conditions.

Increased Efficiency

Data and analytics can also help businesses streamline their operations and improve efficiency. For example, businesses can use data analysis to identify bottlenecks in their processes, leading to process improvements and increased efficiency. Additionally, businesses can use predictive analytics to forecast future market trends and demand, allowing them to better plan their operations and make more informed decisions.

Competitive Advantage

Data and analytics can also provide businesses with a competitive advantage, allowing them to differentiate themselves from their competitors. Companies that are able to effectively use data and analytics to drive growth are more likely to succeed in today's competitive business environment. Additionally, businesses that harness the power of data and analytics are better equipped to stay ahead of the curve and respond to changing market conditions.

Data and analytics play a critical role in driving business growth and success. By using data and analytics to inform decision-making, improve customer understanding, increase efficiency, and gain a competitive advantage, businesses can build a roadmap for success and remain relevant in today's fast-paced business environment.

The future of business growth is an exciting and rapidly changing landscape. The use of technology and digital transformation, the importance of customer experience, and the rise of sustainable business practices are just a few of the trends that are shaping the future of business growth. By staying ahead of the curve and adapting to these changes, businesses can position themselves for long-term success. Whether you're looking to invest in technology, prioritize customer satisfaction, or adopt sustainable practices, the strategies outlined in this blog post can help you grow your business and thrive in the years to come. Remember, the key to success is staying ahead of the game and being proactive in your approach to growth. So, take these predictions and strategies to heart and get ready to propel your business into the future.

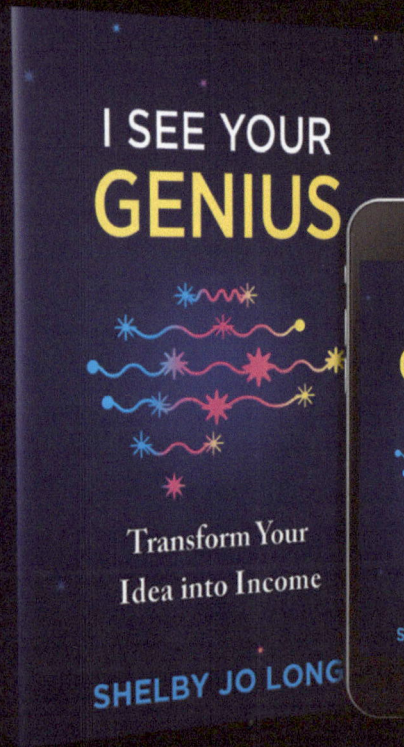
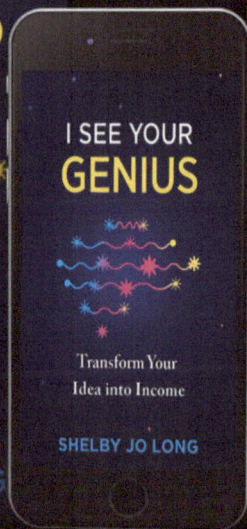

ADVERTISERS